The "How To" Church Effectiveness Study

THE "HOW TO" CHURCH EFFECTIVENESS STUDY
by Tim Passmore

Published by Outcome Publishing
www.gooutcome.com

Second Edition

Printed in the United States of America

1. Religion: Spirituality General
2. Self-Help: Spiritual
3. Christian Life – Personal Growth

Table of Contents

Introduction 5

VISION AND PURPOSE

Session One: The Proper Mindset..........................11

Session Two: The Passion 17

Session Three: The Purpose..................................23

STRATEGY

Session Four: The Plan 29

Session Five: The Position....................................39

Session Six: The Participation 43

LEADERSHIP

Session Seven: The Person 49

Session Eight: The Process 63

Session Nine: The Partnership...............................67

Session Ten: The Program....................................73

End Notes..77

Introduction

Why Do We Need This Training?

He chose David his servant and took him from the sheep pens; from tending the sheep he brought him to be the shepherd of his people Jacob, of Israel his inheritance. And David shepherded them with integrity of heart; with skillful hands he led them.
Psalm 78:70-72

According to Bill McCartney in his book *Blind Spots,*

- 1 percent of churches are growing
- 90 percent of pastors admit they're discouraged.[1]

Leaders Need Help Discovering Blind Spots!

X **O**

We have a blind spot if we don't properly see and address key areas which determine organizational success.

10 Components of Church Organizational Success

1. Members of the church have a ***proper mindset*** concerning the characteristics of a healthy church. Those in the church must measure church health in the same way.

   Question: What are we to produce?

2. Leaders operate the ministries of the church out of a ***passion*** for God. Those in the church must be passionate about obeying God and not self?

   Question: What does God want?

3. Members of the church understand their ***purpose***. Those in the church must know the purpose of the organization and why it's important.

   Question: Is our purpose clear and measurable and do I want to see it fulfilled?

4. Leaders in the church develop a ***plan*** of ministry to accomplish God's purposes. Those in the church must know the plan to accomplish the organizations purpose.

   Question: Do church participants know the plan established to accomplish the purpose?

5. Leaders determine the spiritual ***position*** of people who are associated with the church. Leaders must know where people are in their progression toward becoming servants.

   Question: Where are the people that I lead?

6. Leaders of the church determine how others ***participate***. Church participants must know the importance of those who make up the body of Christ, seeing where people fit into the life of the church.

   Question: Why do people need to serve?

7. Leaders involve each ***person*** as servants, helping them discover their strengths. Those in the church must know their gifts and abilities and serve from their strengths.

   Question: Are people serving from their strengths?

8. Leaders develop a ***process*** of clear communication. Those in the church must know the importance of communicating effectively with one another and between ourselves and God.

   Question: Are we communicating in an effective way with our community, one another, and God?

9. Leaders ***partner*** together with others as a team. Those in the church must have a spirit of cooperation, helping others become successful.

   Question: Are we a team?

10. Leaders develop a *program* of ministry that will bring glory to God. Leaders must be disciplined and accountable to one another to accomplish #s 1-9.

    Question: Are our leaders committed to accomplishing the components that lead to organizational success?

The Blueprint for Effective Organizations

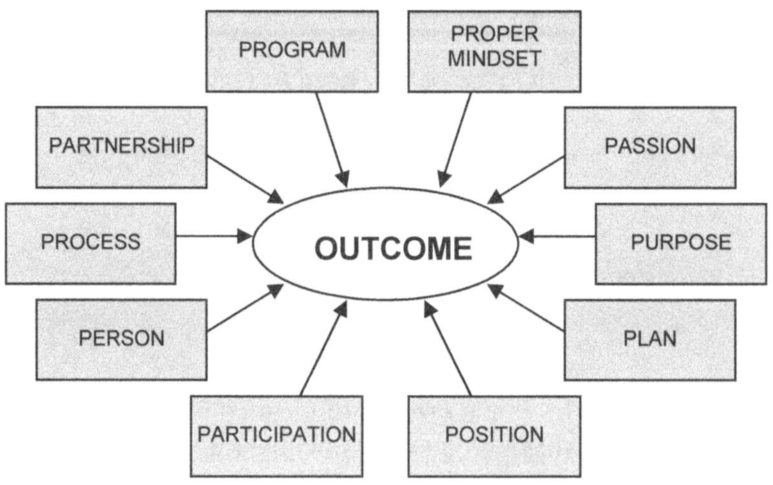

VISION AND PURPOSE

Session One
THE PROPER MINDSET

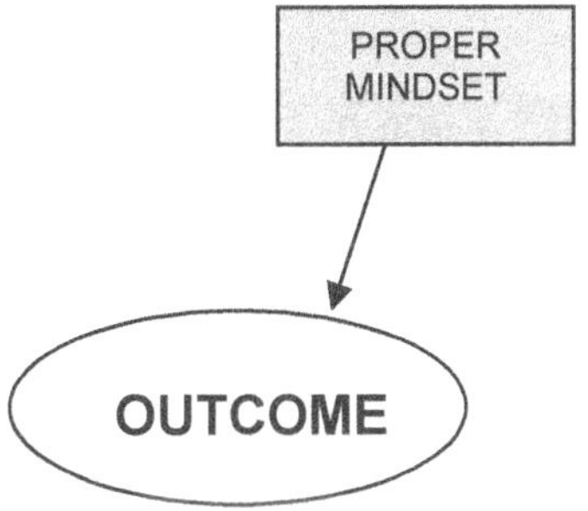

Effective Churches…

Have a ***proper mindset*** concerning the characteristics of a healthy church.

Five Key Truths About Church Health

1. A Healthy Church is a ________________
   ________________.

- ____________ = the body of Christ.

"*Now you are the body of Christ, and each one of you is a part of it.*"
1 Corinthians 12:27

- ____________ = freedom from disease allowing proper function.

- Healthy Church = the body of Christ functioning as Christ's body. The body of Christ functions when the parts of the body fulfill their roles to serve others.

"Now the body is not made up of one part but of many. [15]If the foot should say, "Because I am not a hand, I do not belong to the body," it would not for that reason cease to be part of the body. [16]And if the ear should say, "Because I am not an eye, I do not belong to the body," it would not for that reason cease to be part of the body. [17]If the whole body were an eye, where would the sense of hearing be? If the whole body were an ear, where would the sense of smell be? [18]But in fact God has arranged the parts in the body, every one of them, just as he wanted them to be. [19]If they were all one part, where would the body be? [20]As it is, there are many parts, but one body. [21]The eye cannot say to the hand, "I don't need you!" And the head cannot say to the feet, "I don't need you!" [22]On the contrary, those parts of the body that seem to be weaker are indispensable, [23]and the parts that we think are less honorable we treat with special honor. And the parts that are unpresentable are treated with special modesty, [24]while our presentable parts need no special

treatment. But God has combined the members of the body and has given greater honor to the parts that lacked it, [25]so that there should be no division in the body, but that its parts should have equal concern for each other. [26]If one part suffers, every part suffers with it; if one part is honored, every part rejoices with it. [27]Now you are the body of Christ, and each one of you is a part of it."
1 Corinthians 12:14-27

- The health of the church is measured by the number of people who are using their gifts in ________ _____ ______________.

  What percentage of people in your church are involved in service? ____________

- The fruit of our lives is service and service is evidence of our spiritual condition. (John 15:5-8).

"I am the vine; you are the branches. If a man remains in me and I in him, he will bear much fruit; apart from me you can do nothing. [6]If anyone does not remain in me, he is like a branch that is thrown away and withers; such branches are picked up, thrown into the fire and burned. [7]If you remain in me and my words remain in you, ask whatever you wish, and it will be given you. [8]This is to my Father's glory, that you bear much fruit, showing yourselves to be my disciples."
Jesus
John 15:5-8

- We've been prepared by God to fulfill our roles. It's ______ _______ ____________ God is looking for. We are saved to serve!

"*For it is by grace you have been saved, through faith—and this not from yourselves, it is the gift of God—not by works, so that no one can boast." For we are God's workmanship, created in Christ Jesus to do good works, which God prepared in advance for us to do.*"
Ephesians 2:8-10

2. A healthy church is a _________________ ____________, not a cancerous church.

"*I sometimes think of the human body as a community, and then of its individual cells such as the white cell. The cell is the basic unit of an organism; it can live for itself, or it can help form and sustain the larger organism….* A cell… "*can be part of the body as a loyalist, or it can cling to its own life. Some cells do choose to live in the body, sharing its benefits while maintaining complete independence – they become parasites or cancer cells…. In exchange for its self-sacrifice, the individual cell can share in what I call the ecstasy of community. No scientist can yet measure how a sense of security or pleasure is communicated to the cells of the body, but individual cells certainly participate in our emotional reactions…. If you look for a pleasure nerve in the human body, you will come away disappointed; there is none. There are nerves for pain and cold and heat and touch, but no nerve gives a sensation of pleasure. Pleasure appears as a by-product of cooperation by many cells.*"[2]
Dr. Paul Brand, In The Likeness of God

The Four Types of Cells:

- ________________ Cell = They don't notice people who are lost. They only see themselves. They say: I don't like….
- _______-________________ Cell = They are moving toward becoming cancerous cells. They notice those who are lost, and know they should do something to reach them, but don't.

  They say: I know people need Jesus, but….
- _______-________________ Cell = They are moving toward becoming a functional cell. They notice those who are lost pray for them, and ask God to reveal His plan of ministry. They don't follow the plan.

  They say: I really do want to help, but…
- ________________ Cell = They notice the lost, pray for the lost, ask God to reveal His plan of ministry, and work to fulfill that plan.

  They say: I'll do whatever it takes to reach those who are lost.

EXERCISE: Next to each cell type below, take your best guess and write down the percentage of people in your church who fit each description.

- Cancerous Cell = __________
- Pre-cancerous Cell = ___________
- Pre-functional Cell = __________
- Functional Cell = __________

3. A healthy church is a ___________________ _____________.

(See pages 23-26 in *The Effective Church*)

- The church that is balanced does not focus on only one area of ministry.

A Look at All Participants in the Church

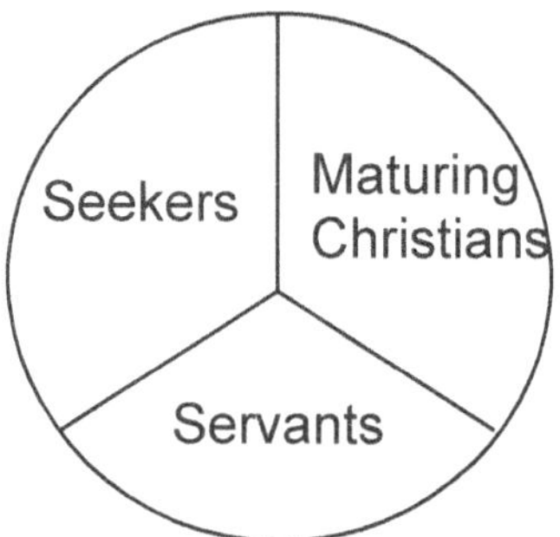

EXERCISE: Next to each category in the pie chart, take your best guess and write down the percentage of people in your church who are described by each category.

Session Two

THE PASSION

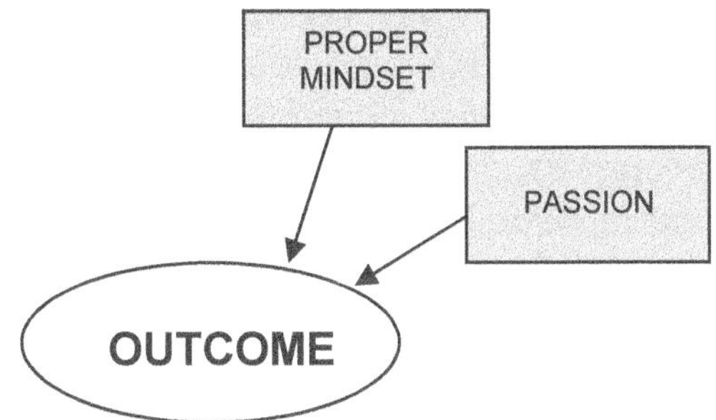

Effective Churches…

Operate the ministries of the church out of a ***passion*** for God.

Leading and Living Out of a Heart for God

"I thank you all so much for your prayers and support. Surely your reward in heaven will be great. Thank you for investing in my life and spiritual wellbeing. Keep sending missionaries out. Keep raising up fine young pastors. In regards to any service, keep it small and simple. Yes, simply, just preach the gospel... Be bold and preach the life-saving, life-changing, forever-eternal gospel. Give glory and honor to the Father. The Missionary heart: Care more than some think is wise; risk more than some think is safe; dream more than some think is practical; expect more than some think is possible. I was called not to comfort or success but to obedience... There is no joy outside of knowing Jesus and serving him."[3]
Karen Watson

A Choice of the Heart

- Our hearts will do one of two things: they will ___________ _____ _____ __________ ______!

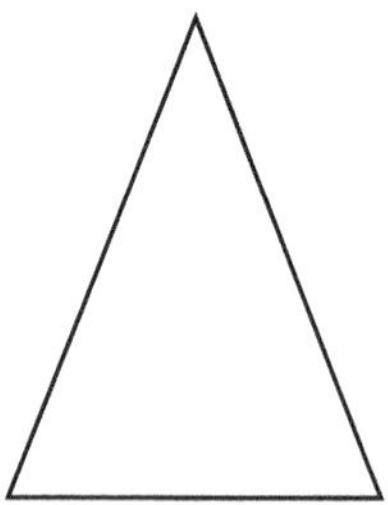

- A passion for God results in ____________.

- We become _____________ when we agree to agree ________ ________.

Ministries Hang on the Commands

Jesus replied: "Love the Lord your God with all your heart and with all your soul and with all your mind. This is the first and greatest commandment. And the second is like it: Love your neighbor as yourself. All the law and the Prophets hand on these two commandments."
Matthew 22:37-40

The commands are to love the Lord and to love others. Everything we do in the church are to hang on these two commands. We are to ask…

- Does the ministry show our love for _________?

- Does the ministry show our love for _____________?

We are not commanded to do things that show love for ourselves. Unfortunately, many times we hang on to ministries that we like instead of performing ministries that make a difference. The ministries we perform have to do with the attitudes of our hearts. Look at the four truths that are listed below.

- The evidence of our passion for God is _________________. A heart of sacrifice is recognized through a "whatever it takes" attitude.

The Passion

To the weak I became weak, to win the weak. I have become all things to all men so that by all possible means I might save some.
1 Corinthians 9:22

- A heart of sacrifice leads to a willingness to _____________.

- Leaders in the church must determine if ministries are _______________ _____ ________ or activities which lead others to follow the commands of God.

- The church was not established to be an institution, but a __________________.

Exercise: Answer the following questions. (Questions from Michael J. Wilkins' book *In His Image).*[4]

- Are we making people into disciples of our institutions, or are our institutions making people into disciples of Jesus?

- Are our disciples proficient at running programs, or at living a real relationship with Jesus?

- Does our attachment to our institutions isolate us from the world, or equip us for changing the world?

- Are people focusing on us because of the importance of our programs or are we (and our programs) the "means to the end," so people see Jesus more clearly?

Exercise: What ministries in your church are ineffective? What should you do about them?

A Willingness to Change

- A willingness to change begins with ______________.

- A willingness to change requires ______________ _________________.

"*A great ministry to the unchurched does not just happen. Such a ministry is not only the result of a clear, thoughtful and well-articulated philosophy but also a commitment to adequate preparation of the congregation. The pastors of these churches have worked long and hard to get people in the right frame of mind so that the ministry is not a bunch of programs, but a group of loving people who really care about the spiritual health of others.*"[6]

George Barna

Session Three
THE PURPOSE

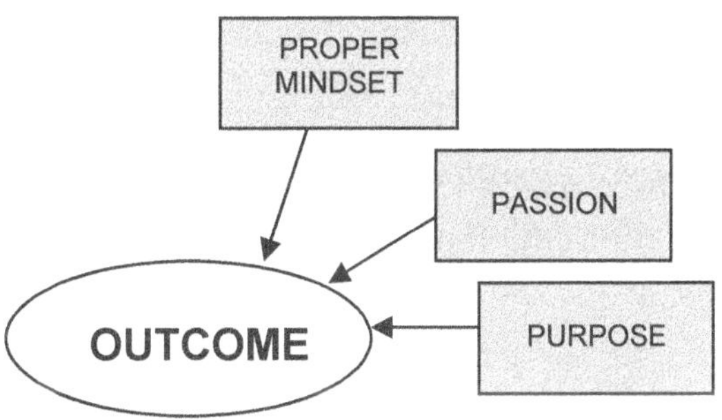

Effective Churches…
Understand their ***purpose***.

Mission Control

- The church is a ______________ ____________________. Those in the church are missionaries, which means, we are on a mission.
- The Church Mission Control Team is responsible for defining the mission of the church and to make certain that the mission is __________ ____________________.
- The purpose of the church determines the mission of the church and provides a way to _____________ ______ ____________________.

(See pages 45-50 in *The Effective Church* for more information about the significance of purpose).

The Purposes of the Church

> *They devoted themselves to the apostles' teaching and to the fellowship, to the breaking of bread and to prayer. Everyone was filled with awe, and many wonders and miraculous signs were done by the apostles. All the believers were together and had everything in common. Selling their possessions and goods, they gave to anyone as he had need. Every day they continued to meet together in the temple courts. They broke bread in their homes and ate together with glad and sincere hearts, praising God and enjoying the favor of all the people. And the Lord added to their number daily those who were being saved.* (Acts 2:42-47).

Our God Determines Our Purpose

- Worship –
- Fellowship –
- Evangelism –
- Discipleship –
- Ministry –

(See pages 51-52 in *The Effective Church*, for other definitions)

A Statement of Purpose

- An effective purpose statement includes ______ ________________ that are to be accomplished.
- An effective purpose statement is ___________. People understand what it means and what they are to do.
- An effective purpose statement is _______________. People have a desire to accomplish it because of the benefit it produces when accomplished. They believe it is worth their sacrifice.
- An effective purpose statement is _______________. People can easily tell if they are successful and are willing to be held accountable to the goals set forth.

Exercise: What is your purpose? Write it in the space provided below. If you don't have a purpose, brainstorm what this purpose statement might be.

STRATEGY

Session Four
THE PLAN

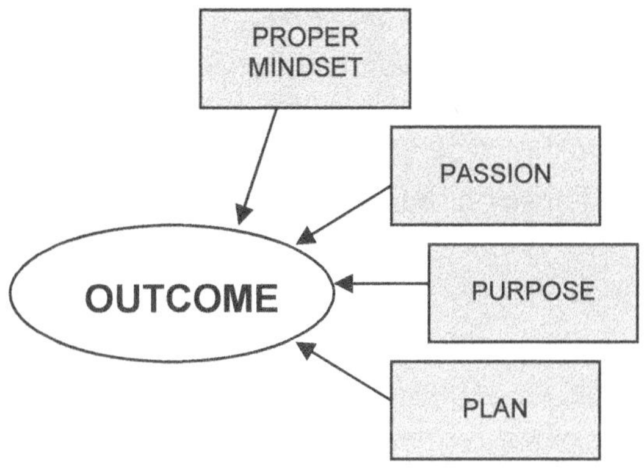

Effective Churches…

Develop a ***plan*** of ministry to accomplish God's purposes.

A Plan For Moving People Closer to God

A plan is "a scheme for making, doing, or arranging something..."[8]

The Four P's of organizational success:

- *There must be a* _________ ________________
- *People must have a clear picture of what it is to do*
- *There must be* ___ __________
- *People must have a part to play.*[9]

Those on the Journey

- *A* _______________ = someone who is searching. There are three types of seekers.
    - *The Christian Seeker* = We seek those who are lost so they may be saved. Jesus is our example. He came to seek and to save what was lost. We are not Christ-like until we become Christian Seekers. He succeeded by identifying the lost and showing His love through service. Jesus said, "*For the Son of Man came to seek and to save what was lost.*" (Luke 19:10).

    - *The Non-Christian Seeker from a Christian Home*. They don't have a relationship with God and are seeking to fill the void in their lives. Quite often they understand the traditions and the language of the church.

- *The Non-Christian Seeker from a Non-Christian Home*. They don't have a relationship with God and are seeking to fill the void in their lives. They don't understand the traditions or the language of the church.

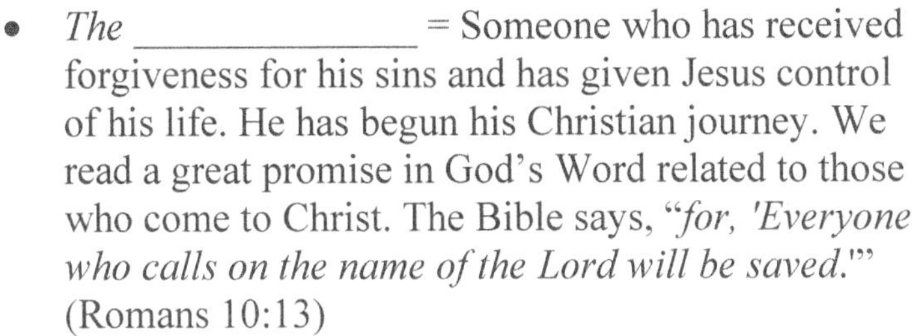

- *The* _____________ = Someone who has received forgiveness for his sins and has given Jesus control of his life. He has begun his Christian journey. We read a great promise in God's Word related to those who come to Christ. The Bible says, "*for, 'Everyone who calls on the name of the Lord will be saved.'*" (Romans 10:13)

- *The* _____________ = someone who has matured in his Christian faith to the point that he has discovered his spiritual gifts and has begun using his gifts in acts of ministry. Jesus said, "*Now get up and stand on your feet. I have appeared to you to appoint you as a servant and as a witness of what you have seen of me and what I will show you.*" (Acts 26:16)

from seeker to servant

mapping "purpose"

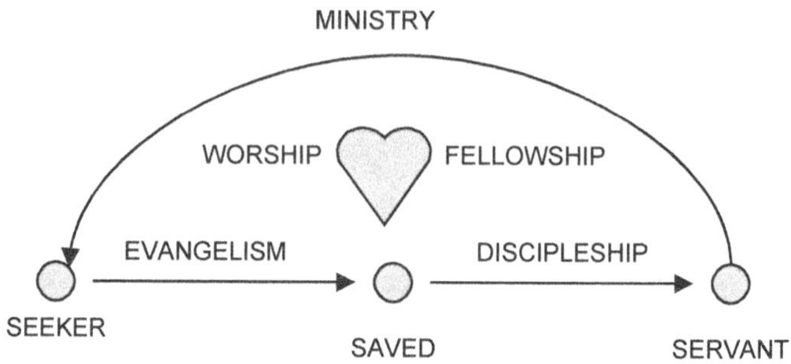

location points

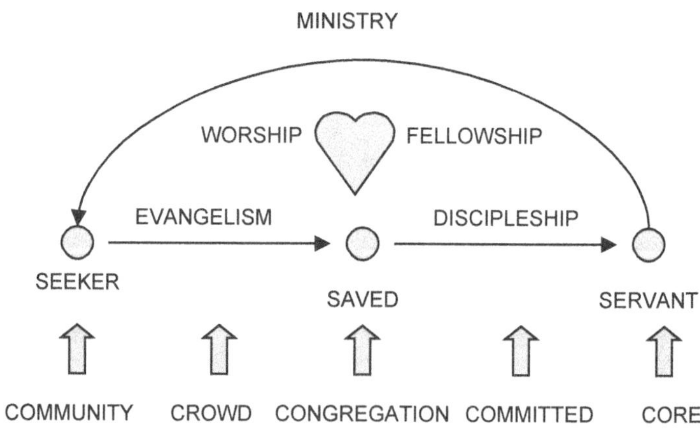

The Location Points

- *Community* = Unchurched. Those in this group include unsaved individuals living in the ministry area of the church.
- *Crowd* = Attenders. Those in this group consist of the unsaved who have made a connection to the local church.
- *Congregation* = Members. Those in this group are individuals who have received Christ as their Savior and who have publicly professed him as Lord through baptism.
- *Committed* = Maturing Members. Those in this group are individuals who have begun maturing in their faith by practicing the disciplines of the faith.
- *Core* = Lay Ministers. Those in this group include individuals who have discovered their spiritual gifts and who have begun using their gifts in acts of service.

Mapping Ministries

We can also map the ministries we perform to accomplish the purposes of the church. You can find a description of these ministries in the The Effective Church book on pages 64-76.

The Plan

mapping ministries

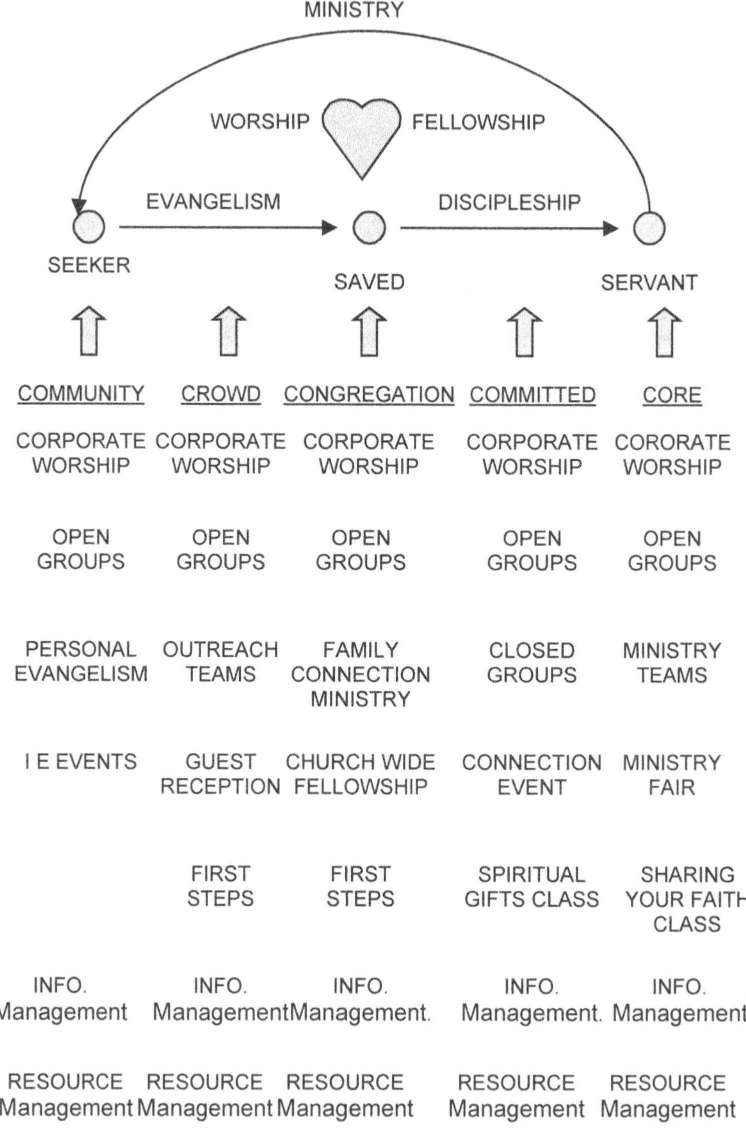

EXERCISE: In the “mapping ministries” diagram above, circle the ministries that you do not currently have or, if you do have them, aren’t functioning in a healthy way.

EXERCISE: What ministries are you doing that are not on the map? Where would you put them? Put them on the map!

BRAINSTORM SESSION
Under each heading, write down what you’d like to do to fulfill the purpose of the church through that ministry.

Corporate Worship:

Intentionally Evangelistic Events:

The Plan

Open Groups:

Outreach:

Closed Groups:

Family Connection Ministry:
(Deacons or Care Leaders)

The Plan

Missions:

New Member Training:

Fellowships:

Other:

EXERCISE: On the following page, map your ministries.

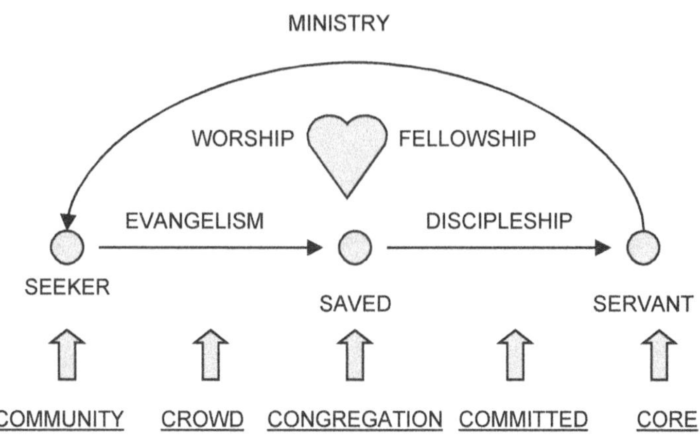
MINISTRY
WORSHIP
FELLOWSHIP
EVANGELISM
DISCIPLESHIP
SEEKER
SAVED
SERVANT
COMMUNITY
CROWD
CONGREGATION
COMMITTED
CORE

Session Five
THE POSITION

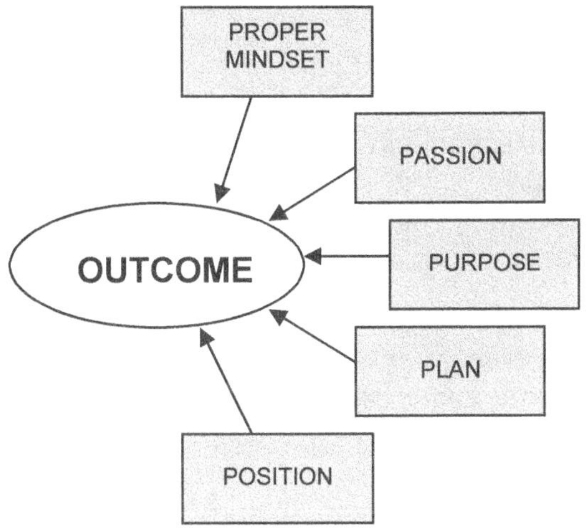

Effective Churches…
Determine the spiritual ***position*** of people who are associated with the church.

The Journey

It's simple! Ask everyone to do three things…

- Come to ______________. This is important to connect with God.
- Be in a __________ ____________. This is important to learn about God.
- Have a __________________. This is important to serve God.

The goal of the church is to assist others as they travel from one _________________ ____________ to the next, moving them closer to God.

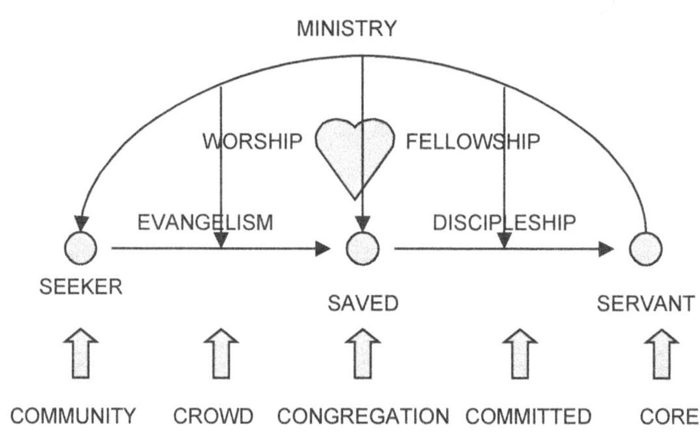

(See pages 82-94 in *The Effective Church* for information on how to map people in the process toward becoming servants*)*

scoring those in the church

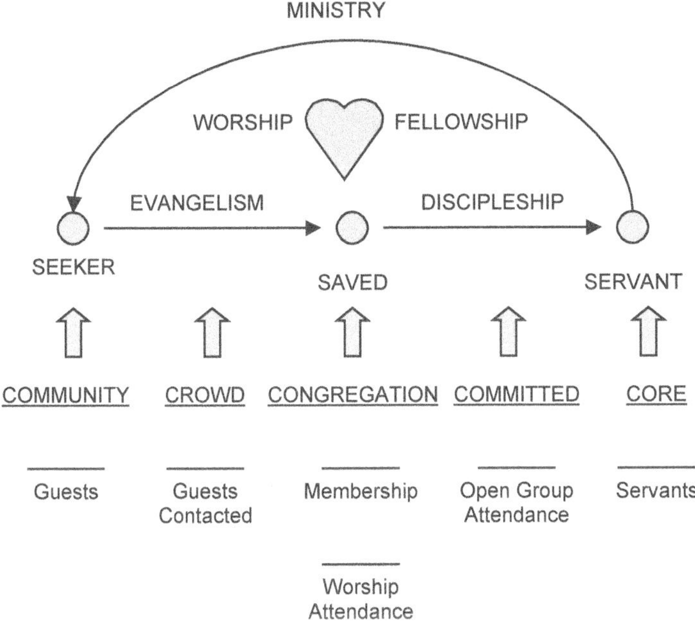

____	____	____	____	____
Guests	Guests Contacted	Membership	Open Group Attendance	Servants
		____		
		Worship Attendance		

scoring those in your ministry

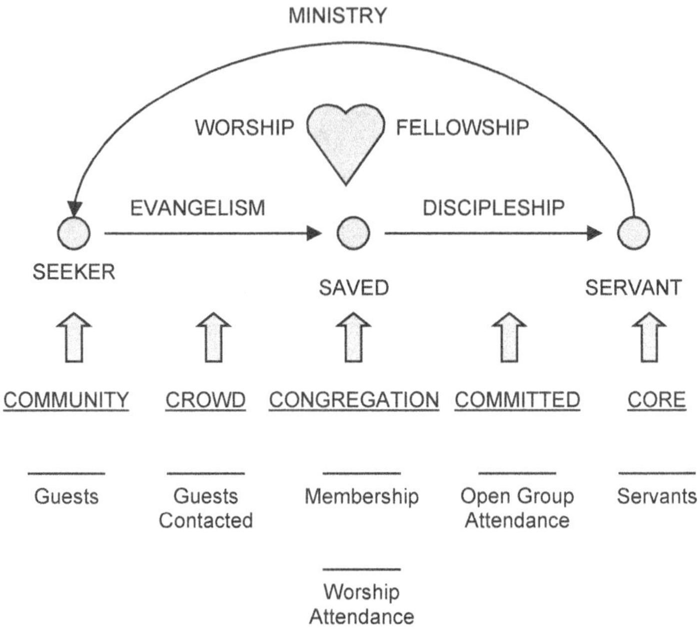

Session Six
THE PARTICIPATION

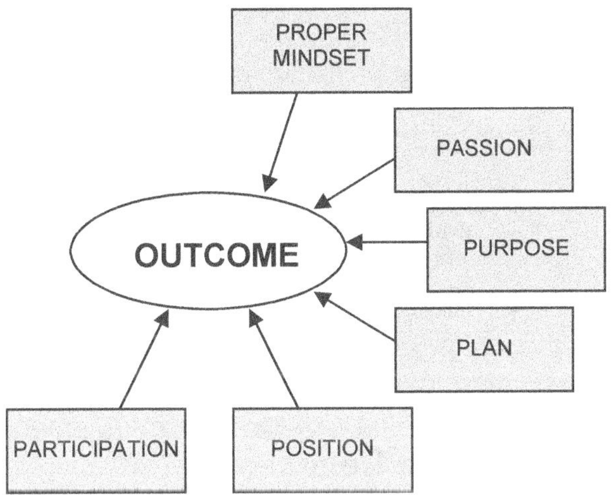

Effective Churches…
Define how leaders will ***participate***.

Principles of Participation

- A plan will work when components of the plan are ___________________.
- A plan will work when components of the plan are implemented.
- Components of the plan are implemented when _____________________ _______ __________.
- Assignments are completed when those assigned responsibilities are capable to perform their tasks.
- Assignments are completed when those assigned understand why their tasks are important.
- Assignments are completed when those assigned _______ _______________ about the outcome.

Divide and Conquer

- Satan's Strategy – _____________________.

Satan wants us to turn on other believers, keeping us from working together to advance God's kingdom. The strategy works. Church after church has experienced division and the result is people missing heaven. He wants us to become turf protectors and concentrate on our own needs rather than the needs of others. War is the result.

"There love and awe at how God was working among them enabled them to introduce thousands of people to Christ every day. I am convinced that if the typical unchurched person were invited to get involved with such a collection of believers – people engaged in the kind of life described in these few verses – they would jump at the opportunity. And why shouldn't everyone have the change? God created us to be involved in such a church. Jesus died so that we might have the opportunity to share that kind of fellowship."[10]
George Barna

- The Church's Strategy – ___ _________ _________.

The church that is healthy operates as a "relay ministry." Leaders pass off people to leaders who have expertise in certain areas in the process of moving people closer to God. This is God's idea of "divide and conquer." We are to divide the responsibilities of ministry among Ministry Partners who are gifted in certain areas and allow them to use their gifts in moving people closer to God. The "divide and conquer" approach allows us to succeed in leading others to become servants of God. The Strategy Map shows us how this is accomplished.

Who's Doing What?

Exercise: Circle those ministries where you are lacking leaders in the diagram on the next page.

The Participation

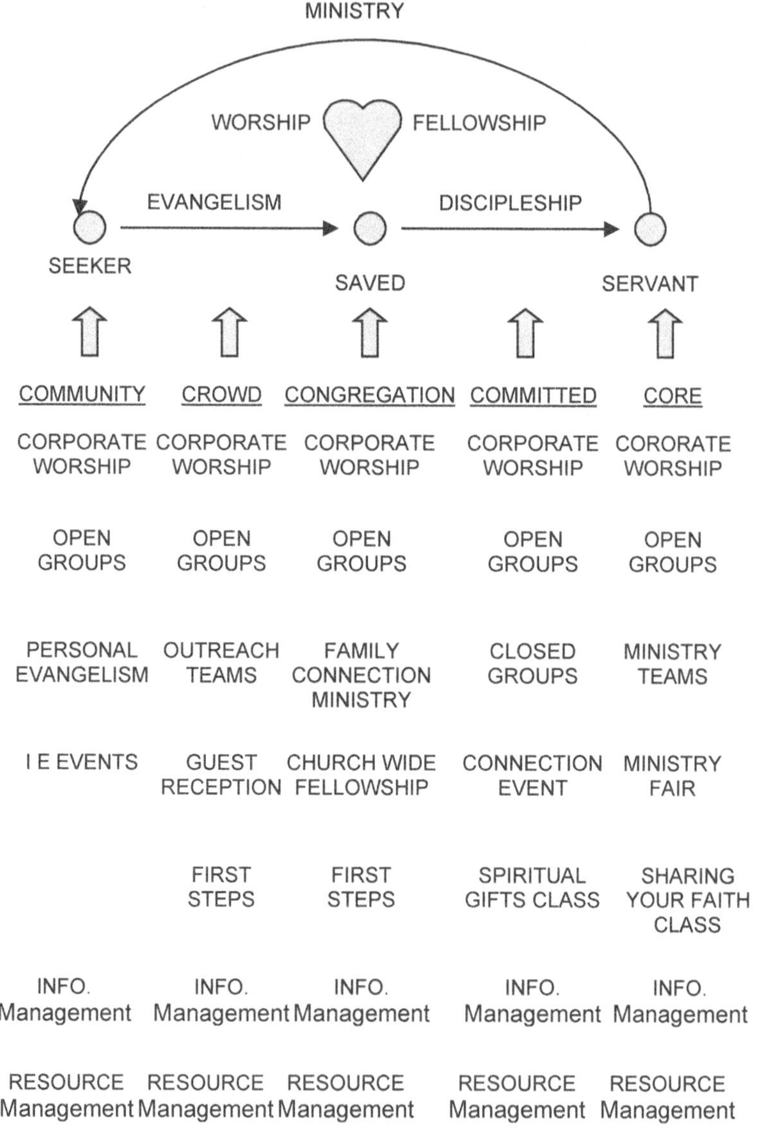

LEADERSHIP

Session Seven
THE PERSON

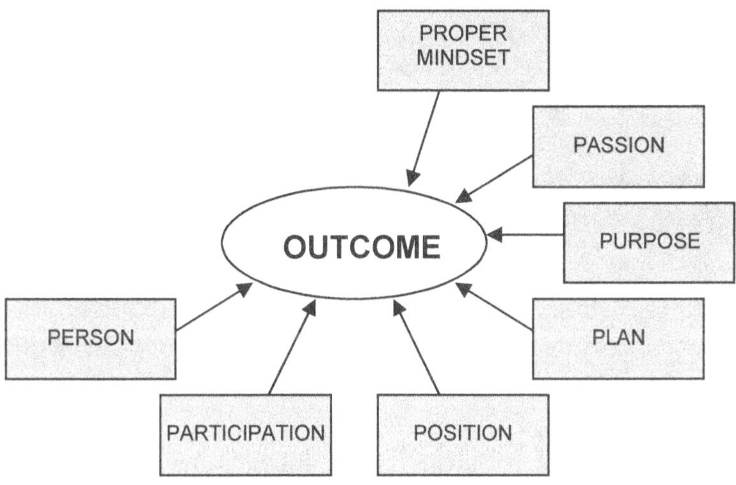

Effective Churches…
Train each ***person*** to be effective in their roles.

The Leadership Diamond

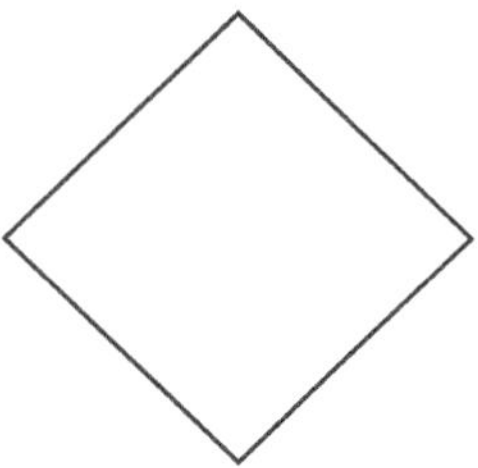

(See page 115 in *The Effective Church* for the illustration and write the leadership areas of emphasis around the diamond)

The Skill of Choosing Leadership Styles

Choosing which golf club to use on the golf course is similar to our choosing a leadership style. The situation dictates to us the leadership style needed. Daniel Goleman, a professor at Harvard, taught about the importance of choosing appropriate leadership styles in a given situation in an article in the Harvard Business Review. He wrote,

> *"...the research indicates that leaders with the best results do not rely on only one leadership style; they use most of them in a given week – seamlessly and in different measure – depending on the business situation. Imagine the styles, then, as the array of clubs in a golf pro's bag.*

Over the course of a game, the pro picks and chooses clubs based on the demands of the shot. Sometimes he has to ponder his selection, but usually it is automatic. The pro senses the challenge ahead, swiftly pulls out the right tool, and elegantly puts it to work. That's how high-impact leaders operate, too."[11]

Leadership Styles

Goleman lists six styles of leadership, defines them, details situations that are appropriate for their use, and points out their general effect on an organization. They are listed below.

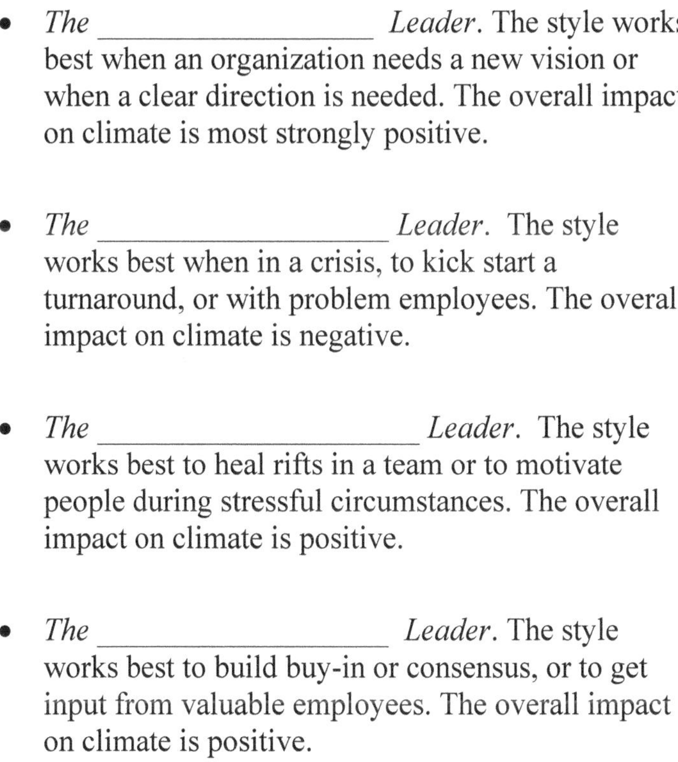

- *The* __________________ *Leader*. The style works best when an organization needs a new vision or when a clear direction is needed. The overall impact on climate is most strongly positive.

- *The* __________________ *Leader*. The style works best when in a crisis, to kick start a turnaround, or with problem employees. The overall impact on climate is negative.

- *The* ____________________ *Leader*. The style works best to heal rifts in a team or to motivate people during stressful circumstances. The overall impact on climate is positive.

- *The* __________________ *Leader*. The style works best to build buy-in or consensus, or to get input from valuable employees. The overall impact on climate is positive.

- *The* ________________________ *Leader*. The style works best to get quick results from a highly motivated and competent team. The overall impact on climate is negative.

- *The* ____________________ *Leader.* The style works best to help an employee improve performance or develop long-term strengths. The overall impact on climate is positive.[12]

(See pages 117-118 in *The Effective Church)*

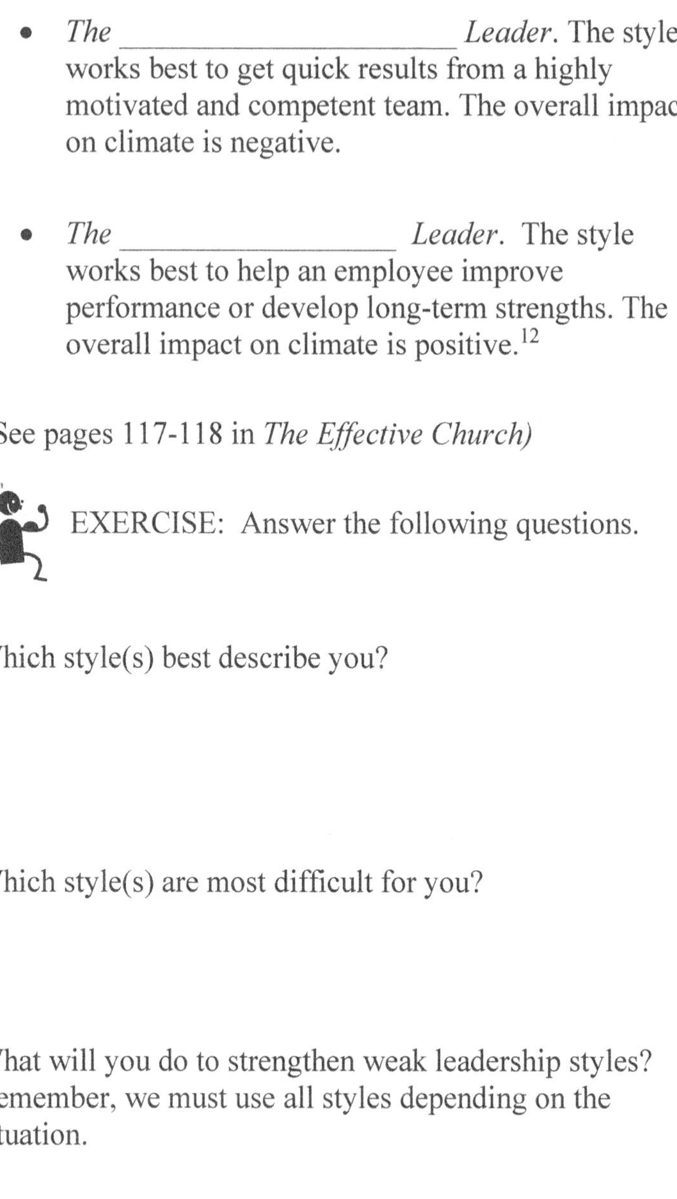

EXERCISE: Answer the following questions.

Which style(s) best describe you?

Which style(s) are most difficult for you?

What will you do to strengthen weak leadership styles? Remember, we must use all styles depending on the situation.

Personal Styles

Choosing the right leadership style for a given situation is critical in leading others to accomplish tasks. Leadership styles are not the only defining qualities that impact our ability to lead. Carlson Learning Systems developed a self administered assessment tool to determine our predominant personal styles. The assessment is known as the DiSC profile.[13] The acrostic relates to four specific personal styles which are defined below. Circle the words and phrases that best describe you.

- ________________________: They are defined by the following words and phrases:
    - Risk takers
    - Determined
    - Decision maker
    - Competitive
    - Problem solver
    - Productive
    - Enjoys challenges
    - Goal driven.

- ________________________: They are defined by the following words and phrases:
    - Energetic
    - Very verbal
    - Spontaneous
    - Friendly
    - Optimistic
    - Thinks out loud
    - Popular
    - Motivates others

- _______________________: They are defined by the following words and phrases:
    - Loyal
    - Avoids confrontation
    - Dislikes change
    - Patient
    - Sympathetic
    - Indecisive
    - Sensitive
    - Not demanding of others

- _____________________: They are defined by the following words and phrases:
    - Accurate
    - Practical
    - Reserved
    - Orderly
    - Factual
    - Likes instructions
    - Detailed
    - Conscientious

(See pages 118-119 in *The Effective Church)*

EXERCISE: Look over the descriptions of personal styles and place a check next to each phrase that describes you.

What two personal styles are predominant?

The Four Fundamental Capabilities

Goleman teaches that leaders have four responsibilities. They are to set strategy; motivate; create a mission; and build a culture."[14] Leaders, according to Goleman, must master four areas called the "fundamental capabilities" for this to occur. These capabilities apply to every leader, whether in a secular or spiritual organization. In the blank next to each description, rate yourself from 0 – 10, 0 = This does not describe me at all and 10 = This completely defines me. They include:

- ________-________________________. The self-aware master the following:
    1. Emotional self-awareness: the ability to read and understand your emotions as well as recognize their impact on work performance, relationships, and the like. _____
    2. Accurate self-assessment: a realistic evaluation of your strengths and limitations. _____
    3. Self-confidence: a strong and positive sense of self-worth. _____

- _________-__________________. Those who practice self-management master the following:
  1. Self-control: the ability to keep disruptive emotions and impulses under control. _____
  2. Trustworthiness: a consistent display of honesty and integrity. _____
  3. Conscientiousness: the ability to manage yourself and your responsibilities. _____
  4. Adaptability: skill at adjusting to changing situations and overcoming obstacles. _____
  5. Achievement orientation: the drive to meet an internal standard of excellence. _____
  6. Initiative: a readiness to seize opportunities. _____

- _______________-_________________. The socially aware master the following:
  1. Empathy: skill at sensing other people's emotions, understanding their perspective, and taking an active interest in their concerns. _____
  2. Organizational awareness: the ability to read the currents of organizational life, build decision networks, and navigate politics. _____
  3. Service orientation: the ability to recognize and meet customer's needs. _____

- _____________ __________. Those who use proper social skill master the following:
  1. They are able to communicate with others in a compelling and understandable way. _____
  2. They have the ability to coach others well as they help develop their skills through their example and instruction. _____
  3. Conflict management: the ability to de-escalate disagreements and orchestrate resolutions.

     _____
  4. Teamwork and collaboration: competence at promoting cooperation and building teams.[15]

     _____

(See pages 119-122 in *The Effective Church)*

EXERCISE: We easily have blind spots in these areas.

1. Ask team leaders about your effectiveness in each of these areas.

2. What will you do to strengthen weak areas?

Leadership Traits

What is God looking for in a leader? Becoming the leader that God desires is the most critical element of becoming a successful leader. There are certain traits that leaders in the church should possess. We discover these traits by focusing on the dialogue that took place between Moses and his father-in-law Jethro. Moses was trying to do everything himself and Jethro wanted to help him by giving him some advice. Jethro confronted Moses and said,

> "*What you are doing is not good. You and these people who come to you will only wear yourselves out. The work is too heavy for you; you cannot handle it alone. Listen now to me and I will give you some advice, and may God be with you. You must be the people's representative before God and bring their disputes to him. Teach them the decrees and laws, and show them the way to live and the duties they are to perform. But select capable men from all the people—men who fear God, trustworthy men who hate dishonest gain—and appoint them as officials over thousands, hundreds, fifties and tens. Have them serve as judges for the people at all times, but have them bring every difficult case to you; the simple cases they can decide themselves. That will make your load lighter, because they will share it with you. If you do this and God so commands, you will be able to stand the strain, and all these people will go home satisfied.*" (Exodus 18:17-23)

The Person

We discover several leadership traits in this passage. Leaders are defined by the following:

- *They are* _________________. The word "capable" means "having the ability or qualities necessary for."[16] Those who were selected to lead were to have the abilities and the qualities necessary to accomplish the needed tasks. Do you have the abilities to do what you have been assigned to do?

- *They fear God.* The word "fear" means "awe; reverence."[17] Those who were selected to lead were to be in awe of God and revere him, having hearts that were committed to Him. Is your heart fully devoted to God?

- *They are* trustworthy. The word "trustworthy" means "dependable and reliable."[18] Those who were selected to lead were to be those who could be trusted and depended upon. Can those around you trust you to follow through on commitments?

- *They teach others to* ____________ _________. Moses had the responsibility of teaching them the decrees and the laws. Those who followed the decrees and laws honored God. Do you base your life on God's instruction found in His Word?

- *They are an example in life*. Moses was to show them the way to live. Are you an example in word and in deed?

- *They teach others how to* ___________ _______ _________. Moses was to show them the duties they were to perform. Do you train others to do the jobs they have been assigned?

- *They select other leaders.* Moses was to recruit others to help him in his tasks. They were to be capable, they were to fear God, and were to be trustworthy. Do you recruit other leaders to assist you in ministry? Are they described by these statements?

- *They appoint others related to their giftedness.* Moses was to appoint leaders over thousands, hundred, fifties, and tens. Those who lead groups must have the appropriate spiritual gifts. Do you appoint leaders according to their giftedness?

- *They* ___________ _________. Moses was there to handle the difficult cases that could not be resolved by those in lower levels of leadership. Do you resolve conflict before it becomes an emergency?

- *They delegate.* Moses was only to handle the difficult cases. He was not to do the jobs of those under him. Do you allow people to do the jobs they have been assigned?

(See pages 122-126 in *The Effective Church)*

Do all of these traits describe you? A healthy church has leaders who are defined by these traits. One way to determine if these traits are true of you is to restate them in a personal manner. Complete the following exercise.

EXERCISE: Circle the number which best describes your mastery of the following leadership traits, 0 meaning you are completely unsuccessful, and 10 meaning you are completely successful.

I am capable.

0 1 2 3 4 5 6 7 8 9 10

I fear God.

0 1 2 3 4 5 6 7 8 9 10

I am dependable.

0 1 2 3 4 5 6 7 8 9 10

I teach others to honor God.

0 1 2 3 4 5 6 7 8 9 10

My life is a Godly example for others.

0 1 2 3 4 5 6 7 8 9 10

I teach others how to perform their tasks.

0 1 2 3 4 5 6 7 8 9 10

I select others to assist me in ministry

0 1 2 3 4 5 6 7 8 9 10

I appoint others related to their giftedness.

0 1 2 3 4 5 6 7 8 9 10

I resolve conflict.

0 1 2 3 4 5 6 7 8 9 10

I delegate responsibilities and allow them to do their jobs.

0 1 2 3 4 5 6 7 8 9 10

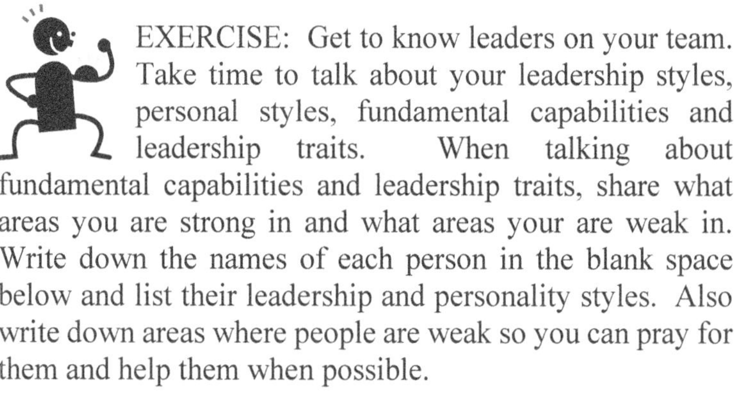

EXERCISE: Get to know leaders on your team. Take time to talk about your leadership styles, personal styles, fundamental capabilities and leadership traits. When talking about fundamental capabilities and leadership traits, share what areas you are strong in and what areas your are weak in. Write down the names of each person in the blank space below and list their leadership and personality styles. Also write down areas where people are weak so you can pray for them and help them when possible.

Session Eight

THE PROCESS

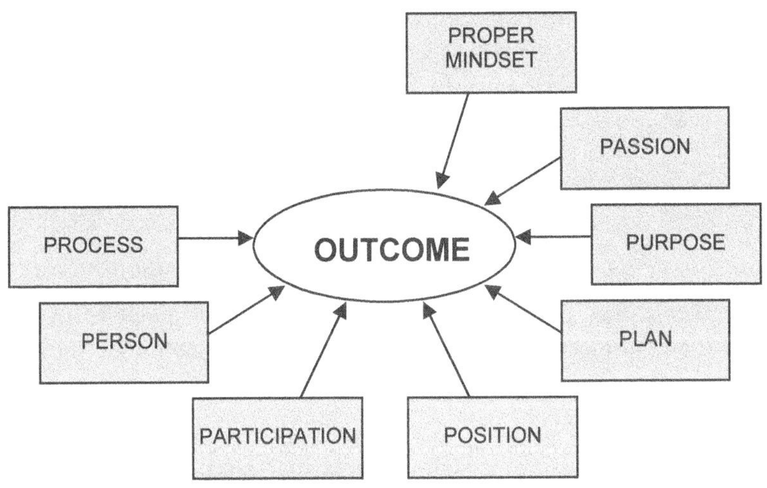

Effective Churches…
Have a ***process*** of clear communication.

Targeting Principles

- A church's target is that group of people which you are aiming to reach.
- Every church has a target.
- Some churches target ________________.
- Some churches target __________________.
- Our target is determined by the ____________ we use. To change your target, change the way you communicate.
- Our target is determined by the ________________ we perform. To change your target, change the way you perform ministry.

How Do We Target?

- Target audiences are reached through ____________ _______________. The principles stated above also apply to these ministries.
- Target audiences are reached through __________ ____________. The principles that apply to segment ministries also apply to small group ministry.
- Target audiences are reached through communication style (_______________).

What are other ways we can target?

EXERCISE: Who are you targeting through your segment ministries, small groups, and worship? Is it believers, non-believers, or both

The Process of Communicating Your Message

Defining the target is not enough. We must communicate the message to them in an understandable way.

The Communication Process

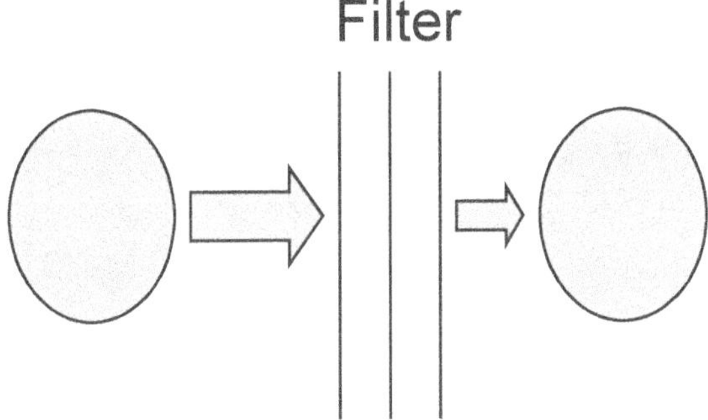

(See page 132 in *The Effective Church)*

The diagram reveals two individuals. There is a sender and a receiver. The message is represented by the arrows. Notice that the arrow coming from the "Sender" is larger than the arrow on the right side of the filter aiming toward the "Receiver." The receiver filters information through his past experiences, his own moral compass, and his impression about the sender.

Communicating With Your Community

To properly communicate, those who are communicating must understand the primary filters of those in the community. The people who are lost who sit in our Worship Centers filter the messages worship leaders are sending. They filter what they hear through their own preferences of....

- Style - Do I connect _________ ______ _____________? Do I understand what is being communicated?
- Substance – Am I hearing something _________ ______ ____________ _____?

EXERCISE: Take some time to answer the following questions to help you develop a plan of communication to reach your target audience.

- What changes do we need to make to communicate effectively with the target audience we desire to reach? (Worship)
- What ministries do we need to add, modify, or remove to help us meet the needs of those we are trying to reach.
- How will we go about making these changes

Session Nine
THE PARTNERSHIP

Mastering Team Leadership

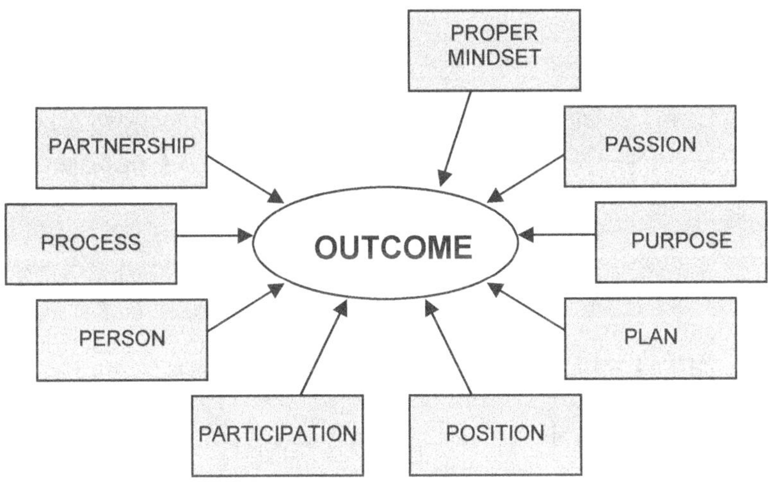

Effective Churches…
Have leaders who ***partner*** together with others as a team.

teamwork

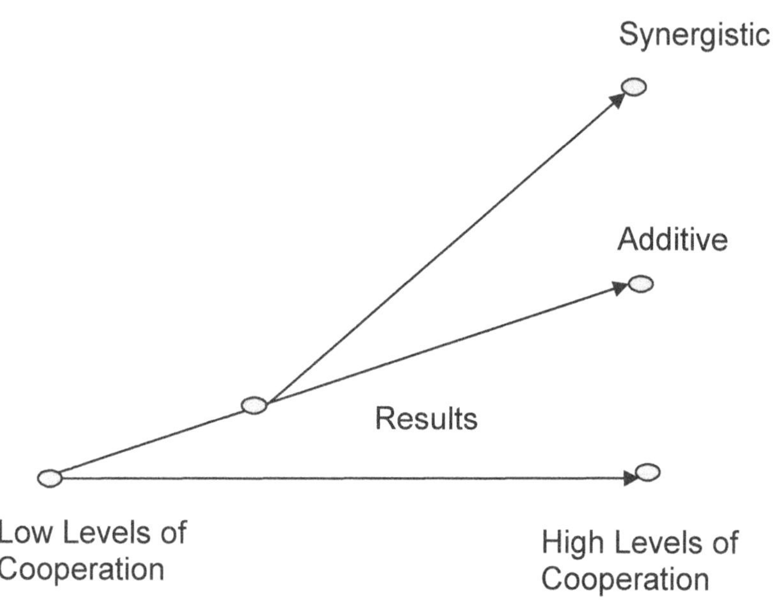

Synergism

A significant difference between a group and a team is their ability to produce multiplied results. This is synergism.

(See pages 145-146 in *The Effective Church)*

Functioning as a Crew

"A clear, common, compelling task that is important to the individual team members is the single biggest factor in team success. All the team workshops in the world pale to insignificance in comparison to a clear and challenging task or goal... When a team is in alignment, every member is highly committed to the team purpose. They are in the same boat, heading in the same direction, pulling together. Alignment provides the focus that unleashes the potential power of the team... When team members are in alignment, they are unified in their intentions. And because they are pulling together in the same direction, there is less wasted energy...."[7]
Pat MacMillan

The crew must be rowing in the same direction for success to be achieved. The crew is heading in a unified direction when these conditions are met. This is illustrated below.

aligning the crew

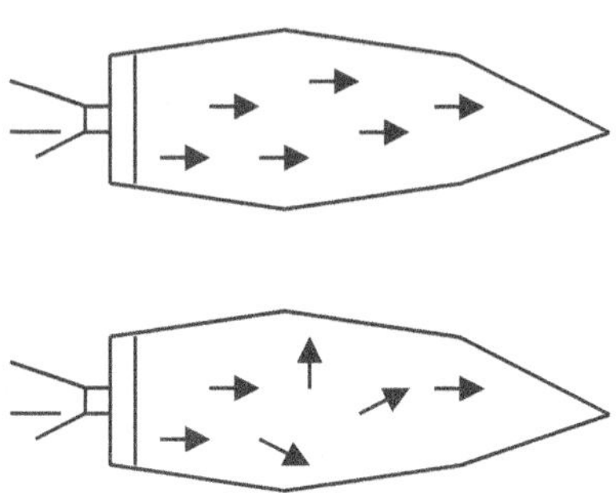

(See pages 146-148 in *The Effective Church*)

EXERCISE: Are the people in your church going in the same direction? If not, why?

MacMillan's Characteristics of a High Performance Team[19]

MacMillan shared six characteristics of teams who achieve synergism. They are illustrated using the following diagram.

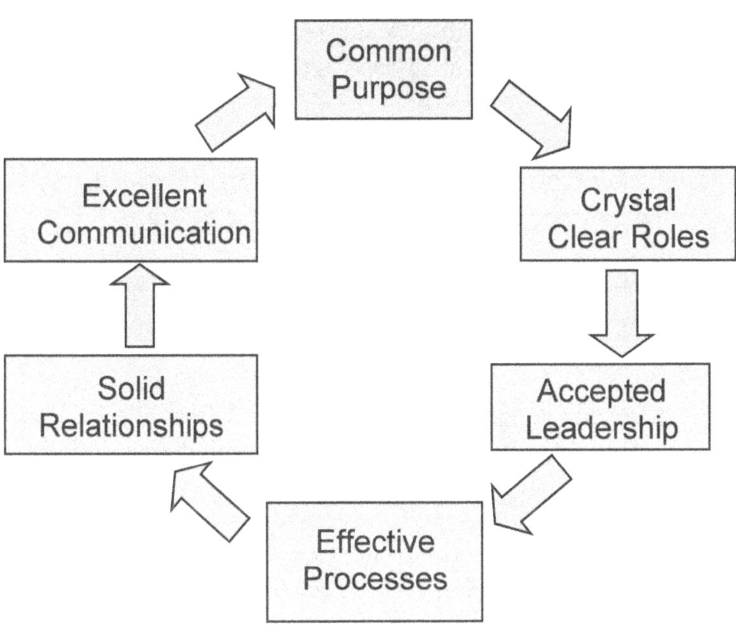

(See pages 149-152 in *The Effective Church)*

 EXERCISE: Answer the following questions?

- Do team members know the purpose and do they agree with it? (If there is no purpose, there is no clear direction).

- Has our team defined the roles people are to play on the team? (Without clear responsibilities, movement toward purpose does not begin)

- Is the leadership of the team accepted? (If the leadership is not accepted, team members will not experience trust)

- Do we have a plan to accomplish our purpose? (Without a playbook, the team will not score)

- Do we, as team members, relate well to one another? (Without respect, teams cannot bond and find synergy)

- Are we communicating our needs and progress well among team members? (Without a clear understanding of needs and progress, accountability can not be accomplished)

Avoiding the Five Dysfunctions

Go to pages 153-155 in *The Effective Church* to learn about The Five Dysfunctions of a Team.

 How would you grade yourself (A,B,C,D or F) on each level of the pyramid?

Session Ten
THE PROGRAM

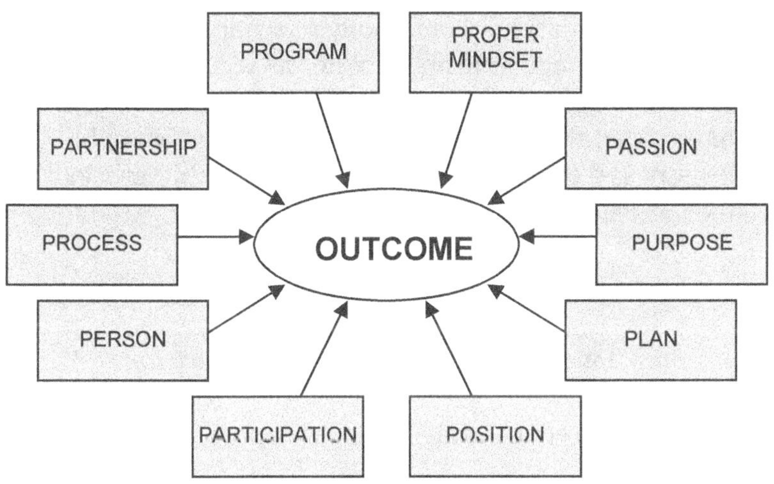

Effective Churches…
Develop a ***program*** of ministry that will bring glory to God.

Combining the Ingredients

The recipe is written, now the ministry must be performed. A strategy is only effective if the people who develop it follow through and make certain that the activities, which have been specified during the planning process, are completed. A healthy church not only has a plan, the leaders work the plan and adjust the plan when the plan is not working. The health of your church is dependent upon your hearing from God and fulfilling His call for the life of the church. This strategy must then be carried out and leaders must hold one another accountable. This is best done in regular team meetings as you evaluate and plan ministries. We should discuss in these meetings if we have added what is necessary of each ingredient to be healthy as a church or ministry in the church. Let's look at the ingredients one more time.

Step One: Begin with the ***proper mind-set***

Step Two: Operate out of the correct ***passion***.

Step Three: Understand your ***purpose***.

Step Four: Create a ***plan*** to accomplish the results God desires.

Step Five: Discover the spiritual ***position*** of others.

Step Six: Lead people to ***participate*** according to their giftedness.

Step Seven: Encourage participants to be the ***people*** (leaders) God desires.

Step Eight: Communicate effectively during the ***process***.

Step Nine: ***Partner*** together as a team.

Step Ten: Develop the ***program*** by combining the ingredients.

EXERCISE: How often is it necessary for your team to meet to evaluate, review upcoming activities, and plan future ministry functions?

EXERCISE: Right now, get out your calendars and plan dates and times for team meetings.

End Notes

Introduction

[1]Bill McCartney, *Blind Spots* (Wheaton, IL: Tyndale House Publishers, Inc.), 13.

Session One

[2] Phillip Yancey, Dr. Paul Brand, *In The Likeness of God* (Grand Rapids, MI: Zondervan, 2004), 35-40.

Session Two

[3]Karen Watson, *Keep Sending Missionaries* (Baptist Press: March 24, 2004), as appears on preachingtoday.com., *Letter from Slain Missionary.*

[4]Michael J. Wilkins, *In His Image* (Colorado Springs, CO: Navpress), 53-54.

[5]M. Scott Boren, *Making Cell Groups Work: Navigating the Transformation to a Cell-Based Church* (Houston: Cell Group Resources, 2002), 89.

[6]George Barna, *Grow Your Church From the Inside Out* (Ventura, CA: Regal Books, 2002), 147.

Session Three

[7]Pat MacMillan, *The Performance Factor: Unlocking the Secrets of Teamwork* (Nashville, TN: Broadman & Holman Publishers, 2001), 44, 46.

Session Four

[8]David Guralnik, *Webster's New World Dictionary* (New York: Simon and Schuster, 1982), 570.

[9]William Bridges, *Managing Transitions: Making the Most of Change* (New York: Perseus Books, 1991), 52-59.

Session Six

[10]Barna, 15.

Session Seven

[11]Daniel Goleman, Daniel, "Leadership That Gets Results," Harvard Business Review (March-April: 2001), 78-80.

[12]Ibid, 82-83.

[13]Barna, 57.

[14]Goleman, 78.

[15]Goleman, 80.

[16]Guralnik, 110.

[17]Ibid, 275.

[18]Ibid, 802.

Session Nine

[19]MacMillan, 36.

[20]Patrick Lencioni, *The Five Dysfunctions of a Team* (San Francisco: Jossey-Bas, 2002), 188.

www.ingramcontent.com/pod-product-compliance
Lightning Source LLC
LaVergne TN
LVHW020656100826
845148LV00012B/2518

9780981509570